METALLICA: CLASSIC SONGS
NOTE-FOR-NOTE TRANSCRIPTIONS WITH DVD

CONTENTS

Transcribed by Howard Fields and Scott Schroedl

Cherry Lane Music Company
Director of Publications/Project Editor: Mark Phillips
Project Coordinator: Rebecca Skidmore

ISBN 978-1-60378-320-0

JUMP IN THE FIRE

Words and Music by
James Hetfield, Lars Ulrich
and Dave Mustaine

1st Verse

Down in the depths_ of my fire - y home,_ the sum-mons bell_ will chime._

Tempt-ing you and all the earth_ to join our sin-ful kind. _ There's a

job to be done___ and I'm the one,___ you peo-ple make me do it.___ Now it's

time for your fate___ and I won't hes - i - tate___ to pull you down in - to this pit. So come on!___

Chorus

Jump in the fire!___

2nd time substitute Drum Pat. 1;
3rd time substitute Drum Pat. 2

So come on!___

Jump in the fire!___

*2nd time play ◆× on
crash & hi-hat on beat 1.

*3rd time play ♪♫
on snare on beat 2.

Drum Pat. 1

Drum Pat. 2

3

4

Coda I

Interlude

3rd Verse

Jump by your will ___ or be tak-en by force, ___ I'll get you ei-ther way. ___

Try-ing to keep the hell-fire lit, ___ I'm stalk - ing you as prey.

Liv-ing your life as me, — I am you you see. — There's

part of me in ev-'ry - one. — So, reach down, grab my hand, — walk with

D.S. al Coda II

me through the land, — come home where you be - long. — So come on! —

Coda II

So come on! —

Jump in the fire! —

So come on! —

Jump in the fire! ____

Outro

Come on,   jump, _ ba - by,   now! ____

Play 3times

*2nd and 3rd times play ♩ on crash on beat 1.

Begin fade

Fade out

FIGHT FIRE WITH FIRE

Words and Music by
James Hetfield, Lars Ulrich
and Cliff Burton

*2nd and 3rd times play on bass drum on beat 1.

1st, 2nd Verses

1. Do___ un - to___ oth - ers___ as___ they've___
2. See additional lyrics

___ done___ to you.___ But___ what___ the___ hell is___

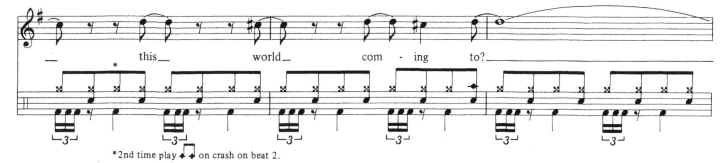

___ this___ world___ com - ing to?_____

*2nd time play ♦♦ on crash on beat 2.

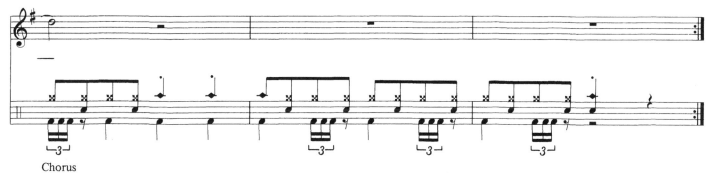

Chorus

Fight fi - re with fi - re.   End - ing is near.

Fight fi - re with fi - re.   Burst - ing with fear.   (Spoken:) We all shall die!

9

3rd Verse

Time_ is _ like_ a fuse,_ short_ and _ burn-ing fast._

_ Ar - ma - ged - don's here,_ like_ said_ in the past._

Chorus

Fight fi - re with fi - re.   End - ing is near.

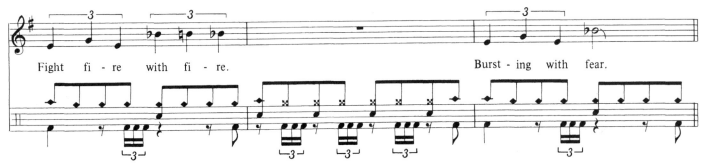

Fight fi - re with fi - re.   Burst - ing with fear.

Half time feel (end half time feel)

Guitar solo

*2nd time play ✦ ✕ on crash and hi-hat on beat 1.

Soon_ to_ fill_ our lungs,_ the_ hot_ winds_ of death._

_ The_ gods_ are_ laugh - ing,_ so_ take_ your_ last breath._

Chorus

Fight fi - re with fi - re. End - ing is near.

Fight fi - re with fi - re. Burst - ing with fear.

Fight fi - re with fi - re. Fight fi - re with fi - re. Fight fi - re with fi - re. Fight fi - re with fi - re.

Fight fi - re with fi - re. Fight fi - re with fi - re. Fight fi - re with fi - re.

Fight fi - re with fi - re. Fight!

Additional Lyrics

2. Blow the universe into nothingness.
   Nuclear warfare shall lay us to rest. *(To Chorus)*

DAMAGE, INC.

Words and Music by
James Hetfield, Lars Ulrich,
Kirk Hammett and Cliff Burton

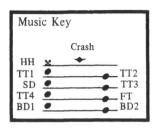

1st, 2nd Verses

1. Deal - ing out the ag - o - ny with - in, charg - ing hard and no one's gon - na
2. Slam - ming through, don't fuck with ra - zor back. Step - ping out, you'll feel our hell on

*2nd time bass drum *2nd time bass drum plays
plays on beat 4. on beat 2.

give in. Liv - ing on your knees, con - form - i - ty, or
your back. Blood fol - lows blood and we make sure.

dy - ing on your feet for hon - es - ty. In - bred, our bod - ies work as
Life ain't for you, and we're the cure. Hon - es - ty is my on - ly ex -

*2nd time bass drum plays
on beat 2.

one, blood - y but nev - er cry sub - mis - sion.
cuse. Try to rob us of it, but it's no use.

*2nd time cymbal line plays

15

Fol - low-ing our in - stinct, not a trend.
Steam-roll - er ac - tion crush-ing all.
Go a - gainst the grain un - til the
Vic -tim is your name and you shall

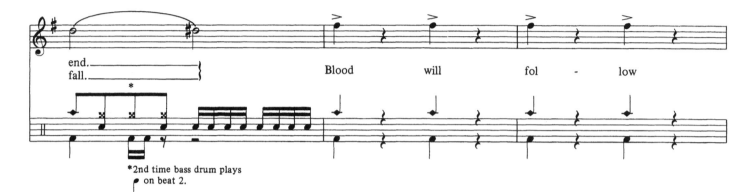

end.
fall.
Blood will fol - low

*2nd time bass drum plays ♪ on beat 2.

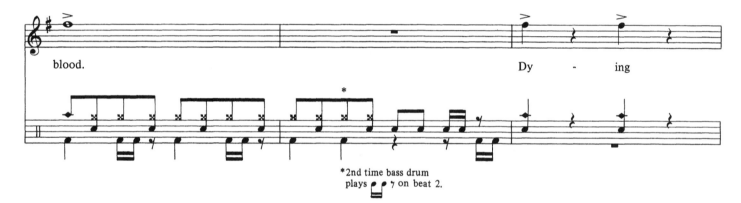

blood.
Dy - ing

*2nd time bass drum plays ♪ ♪ ↱ on beat 2.

time is here.
Dam-age, In - cor - po - rat - ed!

1.

2.
Play 3 times

Bridge

We chew and spit you out. ___ We laugh, you

scream and shout. ___ All flee, with fear you run. ___

You'll know just where we come from.

Dam - age, In - cor - po - rat - ed! *Go!*

Guitar solo

Play 4 times

2nd time bass drum plays ♪♪ on beat 4.

3rd Verse

Dam-age jack-als rip-ping right through you. Sight and smell of this, it gets me

go - ing. Know just how to get just what we want.

Tear it from your soul in night-ly hunt. _____ Fuck it all and fuck-ing no re -

grets.   Nev - er hap - py end - ings on these dark   sets.

All's fair   for Dam - age, Inc., you   see.   Step a lit - tle clos - er if you

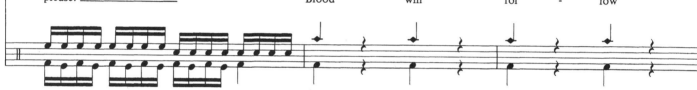

please. _____   Blood will fol - low

blood.   Dy - ing

time   is   here.   Dam - age, In - cor - po - rat - ed!

THE SHORTEST STRAW

Words and Music by
James Hetfield and Lars Ulrich

Double time feel

1st, 2nd Verses

1. Sus - pi - cion is your_ name. Your hon - es - ty to_ blame. Put dig - ni - ty to_ shame.
2. The ac - cu - sa - tions_ fly. Dis - crim - i - na - tion,_ why? Your in - ner self to_ die.

*2nd time bass drum plays on beat 2.

Dis - hon - or.   Witch - hunt, mod - ern_ day.   De - ter - min - ing de - cay.
In - trud - ing.   Doubt sunk it - self in_ you.   Its teeth and tal - ons_ through.

2nd time substitute Drum Pat. 1

The bla - tant dis - ar - ray.   Dis - fig - ure.   The pub - lic eye's dis - grace
Your liv - ing catch two - two.   De - lud - ing.   A mass hys - ter - i - a.

2nd time substitute Drum Pat. 2

De - fy - ing com - mon - place.   Un - end - ing pa - per_ chase.   Un - end - ing.
A meg - a - lo - man - i - a.   Re - veal de - men - ti - a.   Re - veal.

Drum Pat. 1

Drum Pat. 2

22

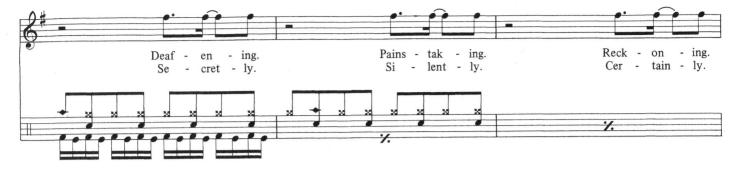

Deaf - en - ing.
Se - cret - ly.

Pains - tak - ing.
Si - lent - ly.

Reck - on - ing.
Cer - tain - ly.

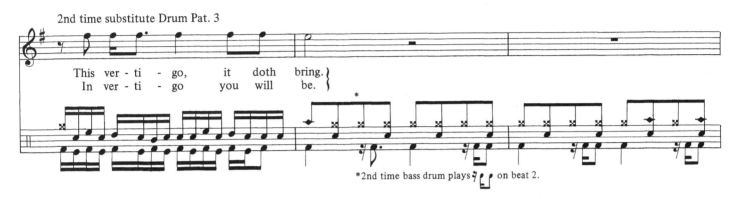

2nd time substitute Drum Pat. 3

This ver - ti - go,   it doth bring.
In ver - ti - go   you will be.

*2nd time bass drum plays on beat 2.

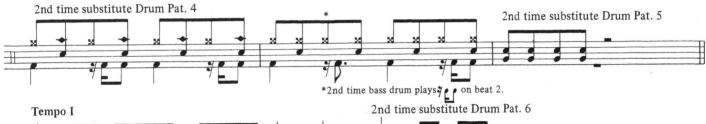

2nd time substitute Drum Pat. 4

2nd time substitute Drum Pat. 5

*2nd time bass drum plays on beat 2.

Tempo I

2nd time substitute Drum Pat. 6

Chorus

Short - est straw.   Chal - lenge lib - er - ty.   Downed by law.

Drum Pat. 3

Drum Pat. 4

Drum Pat. 5

Drum Pat. 6

Live in in - fa - my.   Rub you raw.   Witch - hunt rid - ing through.

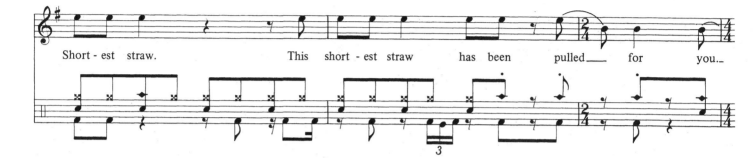

Short - est straw.   This short - est straw has been pulled___ for you.___

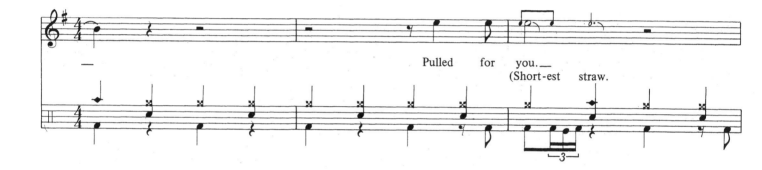

Pulled   for   you.___
(Short - est   straw.

2nd time substitute Drum Pat. 7

Pulled   for   you.
Short - est straw.   Pulled   for

Double-time feel

you.   Short - est straw has been pulled___ for   you.___
Short - est straw.)

Drum Pat. 7

*2nd time bass
drum plays
on beat 3.

2nd time substitute Drum Pat. 8

Guitar Solo I

*2nd time cymbal line plays ⅹ ⅹ on beat 1.

Drum Pat. 8

Chorus

Short - est straw. Chal - lenge lib - er - ty. Downed by law. Live in in - fa - my.

Rub you raw. Witch - hunt rid - ing through. Short - est straw. This

short - est straw has been pulled___ for you.___ Pulled for you.

Double time feel

rit.

28

WHEREVER I MAY ROAM

Words and Music by
James Hetfield and Lars Ulrich

1st, 2nd Verses

2. See additional lyrics

I have stripped of all__ but pride, so in her I do__ con-

*2nd time play on bass drum on beat 4.

fide,__ and she keeps me sat - is - fied.__ Gives me all I need.

And with dust in throat I crave,__ on - ly knowl-edge will I save.__

To the game you stay a slave.__

(end half time feel)

Rov - er,__ wan - d'rer, no - mad, vag - a - bond, call me what you will,__

30

Half time feel

(Whispered:) And the earth be-comes my throne._____ 2. And the earth be -comes my throne._

Coda

speak my mind an - y - where._____ And I'll nev - er mind an - y - where._

Half time feel

Chorus

(end half time feel)

An - y - where I roam,_____ where I lay my head is home,_ yeah!____

Interlude

6

Pre-chorus

But I'll take my time an - y - where.—

I'm free to speak my mind an - y - where.— And I'll re - de - fine an - y - where.

Half time feel
Chorus

An - y - where I roam,——————— where I lay my

head is home.————— Carved up - on—— my stone,———

—— my bod - y—— lie,— but still I—— roam, yeah,— yeah.

Begin fade

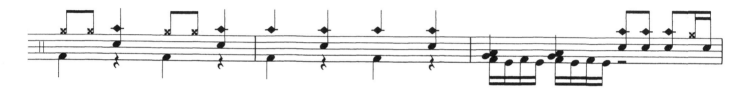

Fade out

Additional Lyrics

2. And the earth becomes my throne,
   I adapt to the unknown.
   Under wandering stars I've grown,
   By myself but not alone.
   I ask no one.
   And my ties are severed clean,
   The less I have, the more I gain.
   Off the beaten path I reign.
   Rover, wanderer, nomad, vagabond,
   Call me what you will. *(To Pre-chorus)*

HERO OF THE DAY

Words and Music by
James Hetfield, Lars Ulrich
and Kirk Hammett

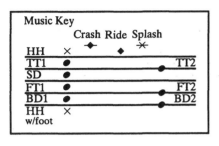

They're off to find— the he - ro— of— the day.—

Mm,— but what if they should fall—— by some - one's wick - ed way?—

———————— Still the win - dow burns,— time so slow - ly turns.—

Some - one there— is sigh - ing. Keep- ers of the flames,— do ya

feel your name?— Can't you hear your— ba - bies cry - in'?————

Ma - ma, they try—— and break—— me.——

Still they try—— and break—— me.——

Half time feel
2nd Verse

Ex - cuse me while—— I tend——

—— to how—— I—— feel.—— These

(end half time feel)

things re - turn—— to me—— that still—— seem real.——

Now, de - serv - ing - ly,_____ this eas - y chair._____

Mm, but the rock - ing stopped_____ by

wheels_____ of_____ de spair._____ Don't want your aid,_____ but the

fist I've made_____ for years_____ can't hold off fear._____ No, I'm

not all me,_____ so please ex - cuse_____ me while I tend_____ to how_____ I feel.

Chorus

But

now the dreams and wak - ing screams that ev - er last the night.
(But now the dreams that ev - er last the night.

So build the wall be - hind it, crawl and hide
So build the wall and hide

un - til it's light.
un - til it's light.)

So can you hear your ba -

Guitar solo

bies cry - in' now?

Still the

3rd Verse

win-dow burns,— time so slow-ly turns.— And some-one there— is sigh-
(The win-dow burns.— Some-one there— is sigh-

ing. Keep-ers of the flames,— can't you hear your names?— Can't you
ing. Keep-ers of the flames.— Can't you

Chorus

hear your ba - bies cry - in'?_____ But now the dreams— and wak-
hear your ba - bies cry - in'?)_____ (But

ing screams— that ev - er last— the— night.— So
now the dreams— that ev - er last— the— night.—

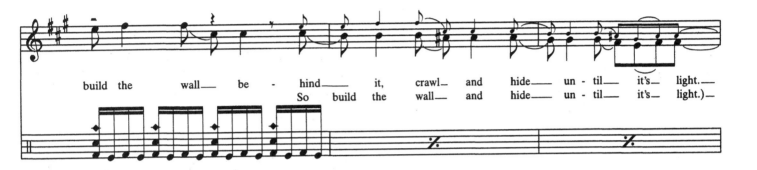

build the wall— be - hind— it, crawl— and hide— un - til— it's— light.—
So build the wall— and hide— un - til— it's— light.)—

— So can't you hear— your ba - bies cry - in' now?—

Outro

Ma - ma, they try— and break—
me.

— me. Ma - ma, they try— and break— me.

Ma - ma, they try____ and break____ me. Ma - ma, they try,____

Ma - ma, they try.____ Ma - ma, they try____ and break____ me.
(Ma - ma, they try____ and break____

Ma - ma, they try____ and break____ me. Ma - ma, they try____ and break____
____ me. Ma - ma, they try____ and break____ me.

____ me. Ma - ma, they try,____
Ma - ma they try____ and break____ me.) Ma - ma, they try,____

Ma - ma, they try._____

slight rit.

THE MEMORY REMAINS

Words and Music by
James Hetfield and Lars Ulrich

mains.

2.

For - tune, fame,__ mir - ror vain,__ gone in - sane...__ Dance,

Bridge

lit - tle tin god - dess.__ Da da da da da da da,

da da da__ da.__ Da da da da da da da,

da da da__ da da. Da da da da da da da.

da　　da　　da＿　da.＿　　　　　Da　da　da　da　　da　da　da,

Chorus

da　　da　　da＿　da＿　da.　　　Drift a - way,＿　fade a - way,＿　lit - tle tin god - dess.＿

Ash　to ash,＿　dust　to dust,　fade　to black.＿

For - tune,　fame,＿　mir - ror vain,＿　gone in - sane...＿

＿＿　For - tune,　fame,＿　mir - ror vain,＿　gone in - sane,＿　but the

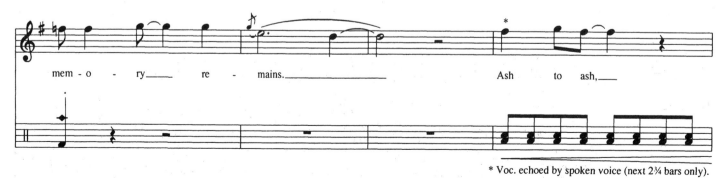

mem - o - ry＿　re - mains.＿　　　Ash　to ash,＿

* Voc. echoed by spoken voice (next 2¾ bars only).

48

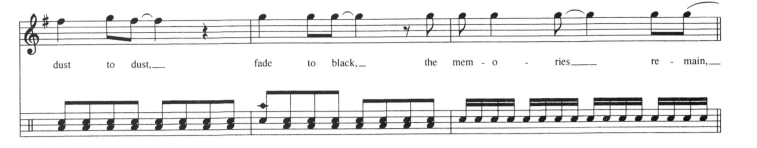

dust to dust,___ fade to black,___ the mem - o - ries___ re - main,___

___ yeah, to this fad - ed pri - ma don -

na, yeah, yeah, yeah, hey, ah.

Guitar solo

Dance, lit - tle tin god - dess, dance.___

Bridge

___ Da da da da da da___ da, da da da___ da.___

da. Da da da da da da da, da da da—— da.——

—— Da da da da da da, da da da—— da—— da. Da da da

da da da———— da, da da da—— da.—— Da da da da da da,

da da—— da—— da. Da da da da da da———— da, da da da—— da.——

—— Da da da da da da da, da da da—— da—— da. Da da da
(Spoken:) Say yes, at least say hello. Say yes,

da da da———— da, da da da—— da.—— Da da da da da da da.
at least say hello. rit.

Additional Lyrics

2. Heavy rings hold cigarettes
   Up to lips that time forgets
   While the Hollywood sun sets
   Behind your back.
   And can't the band play on?
   Just listen, they play my song.
   Ash to ash, dust to dust,
   Fade to black. *(To Chorus)*

FRANTIC

Words and Music by
James Hetfield, Lars Ulrich,
Kirk Hammett and Bob Rock

Intro
Moderately fast Rock ♩ = 168

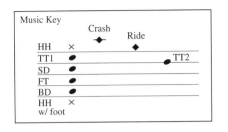

*Hi-hat half-open

Play 8 times

**Play Ride on edge for washy sound.

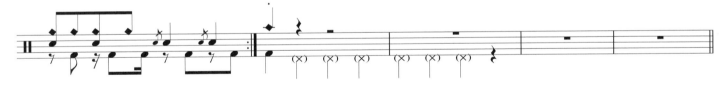

Half-time feel

Verse

1. If I could have __ my wast - ed days __ back, would
   worn out al - ways be - ing a - fraid, an

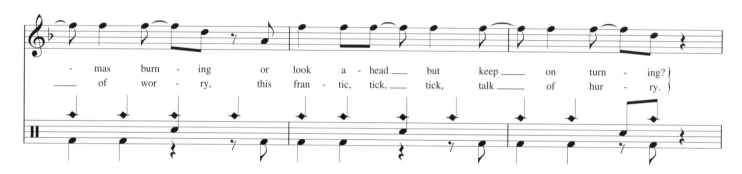

I use them __ to get __ back on __ track, stop to warm __ at kar -
end - less stream __ of fear __ that I've __ made. Tread - ing wa - ter full __

- mas burn - ing or look a - head __ but keep __ on turn - ing?)
  __ of wor - ry, this fran - tic, tick, __ tick, talk of hur - ry.)

Do I have the strength to know how I'll go? __ Can I find it in - side to

deal with what I should - n't know? { Could I have __ my wast - ed days __ back? Would
                                       { Worn out al - ways be - ing a - fraid, an

End half-time feel

I use them __ to get __ back on __ track?)
end - less stream __ of fear __ that I've __ made.)

You live it or lie ____ it! You live it or lie ____ it! (You

live it or lie ____ it! You live it or lie ____ it!)

My life - style de -

ter - mines my death - style. My life - style de - ter - mines my death - style.

𝄋 Pre-Chorus
Half-time feel

Keep search - ing, _____ keep on search - ing. _____

____ This search ___ goes ___ on, ____ { 1., 2. this search ___ goes ___ on. ____
3. on and ___ on. _____

Keep search - ing, _____ keep on search - ing. _____

End half-time feel

This search goes on, _____

1. this search goes on.
2., 3. on and on.

Chorus

Fran-tic, tick, tick,
Fran-tic, tick, tick, tick, tick, tick, tock. Fran-tic, tick, tick,

tick, tick, tick, tock. Fran-tic, tick, tick, tick, tick, tick, tock.

To Coda 1.

Fran-tic, tick, tick, tick, tick, tick, tock!

2. **Interlude**

2. I've tick, tick, tick, tock!

Half-time feel

End half-time feel

Bridge

Do I have the strength to know how I'll go? _____

Can I find it in - side to deal with what I should - n't know? _____

1.

2.

Oh. _____ My life - style de -

(Birth is pain.

ter - mines my death - style, a ris - ing tide that push - es to the oth - er side. My

Life is pain.

life - style de - ter - mines my death - style, a ris - ing tide that

Death is pain. It's all the same.)

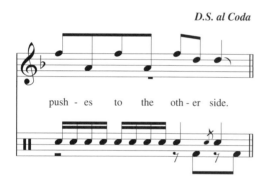

D.S. al Coda

push - es to the oth - er side.

⊕ **Coda**

Outro
Slower ♩ = 128

Play 4 times

tick, tick, tick, tock!